At Home with Science

Munch! Crunch!

What's for lunch?

Written by Janice Lobb
Illustrated by Peter Utton and Ann Savage

KING*f*ISHER

KINGFISHER
Kingfisher Publications Plc
New Penderel House
283-288 High Holborn
London WC1V 7HZ

First published by Kingfisher Publications Plc 2000
10 9 8 7 6 5 4 3 2 1

HB - 1TR/0400/FR/128JWAD
PB - 1BFC(1SBF)/0400/FR/128JWAD

Created and designed by Snapdragon Publishing Ltd
Copyright © Snapdragon Publishing Ltd 2000

A CIP catalogue record for this book is available
from the British Library.

ISBN HB 0 7534 0428 1
ISBN PB 0 7534 0497 4

Printed in Hong Kong

Author Janice Lobb
Illustrators Peter Utton and Ann Savage

For Snapdragon
Editorial Director Jackie Fortey
Art Director Chris Legee
Designers Chris Legee and Rob Green

For Kingfisher
Series Editor Emma Wild
Series Art Editor Mike Buckley
DTP Co-ordinator Nicky Studdart
Production Caroline Jackson

Contents

About this book

Making popcorn in the kitchen doesn't seem like science does it? But it is, and so is watching a loaf of bread rise or making a jelly wobble. This book is about the science that is happening every day in your kitchen. Look around you and you'll be surprised at what you discover.

Where? What if? Which? How? Why?

Hall of Fame

Archie and his friends are here to help you. They are each named after a famous scientist – apart from Bob the duck, who is a young scientist just like you!

Archie
ARCHIMEDES (287–212BC)
The Greek scientist Archimedes worked out why things float or sink while he was in the bath. According to the story, he was so pleased that he leapt out, shouting 'Eureka!', which means 'I've done it!'.

Frank
BENJAMIN FRANKLIN (1706–1790)
This American statesman carried out a famous (but dangerous) experiment in 1752. By flying a kite in a storm, he proved that a flash of lightning was actually electricity. This helped people to protect buildings during storms.

Marie
MARIE CURIE (1867–1934)
Girls did not go to university in Poland, where Marie Curie grew up, so she went to study in Paris, France. She worked on radioactivity and received two Nobel prizes for her discoveries, in 1903 and 1911.

Dot
DOROTHY HODGKIN (1910–1994)
Dorothy Hodgkin was a British scientist who made many important discoveries about molecules and atoms, the tiny particles that make up everything around us. She was given the Nobel prize for Chemistry in 1964.

See for yourself!

1 Read about the science in your kitchen, then try the 'See for yourself!' experiments to discover how it works. In science, experiments try to find or show the answers.

2

Read the instructions for each experiment carefully, making sure you follow the numbered steps in the correct order.

3 Here are some of the things you will need. Have everything ready before you start each experiment.

Deep pan

Measuring jug

Mixing bowl and spoon

Frying pan

Mung beans

Glass jars

Long sock

Tennis ball

Notebook and pencil

Popcorn

Iron nails

Old cutlery

4 # Safety first! ✋

Some scientists have taken risks to make their discoveries, but our experiments are safe. Just make sure that you tell an adult what you are doing, and get their help when you see the red warning button.

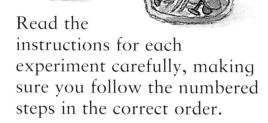

Amazing facts

WOW!

You'll notice that some words are written in *italics*. You can learn more about them from the glossary at the back of the book. And if you want to find out some amazing facts, look out for the 'Wow!' panels.

Look out for useful tips!

Have fun!

Why do I need food?

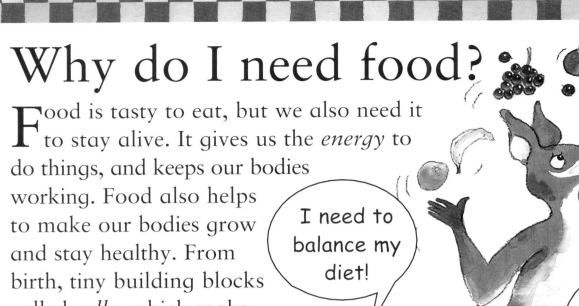

Food is tasty to eat, but we also need it to stay alive. It gives us the *energy* to do things, and keeps our bodies working. Food also helps to make our bodies grow and stay healthy. From birth, tiny building blocks called *cells*, which make up our bodies, have to be repaired and replaced. The *nutrients* we use for this growth and repair come from the food we eat.

I need to balance my diet!

What did the scales say to the sugar?

Energy for life

Green plants use energy from sunlight to make their food.

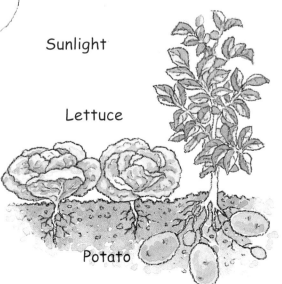

Sunlight

Lettuce

Potato

Lettuce for salads

Potatoes for chips

Unlike plants, we can't produce our own food. We eat food made from plants or animals, and *digest* it to use ourselves.

6

A balanced diet

To stay healthy, we need to eat a mixture of foods which gives us the nutrients our bodies need.

You need *proteins* from foods, such as meat and fish, to build and repair the cells in your body.

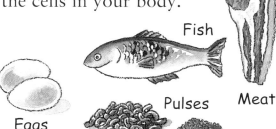

Fish

Eggs

Pulses

Meat

Potato

White bread

Rice

Pasta

Your body needs energy from starchy and sugary foods, called *carbohydrates*, to do things like moving and keeping warm.

Fats also provide energy, and can be stored in the body and used later.

Butter

Oil

Small amounts of *vitamins* and *minerals* keep everything working properly.

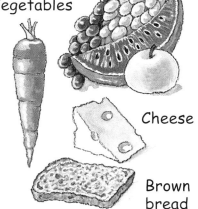

Fruit

Vegetables

Cheese

Brown bread

See for yourself!

1 Try this simple test for fat. Press a piece of food, such as a chip or a piece of cheese, against a thin sheet of paper.

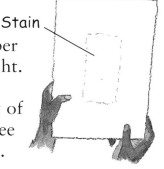

Stain

2 Hold the paper up to the light. If the food contains a lot of fat, you will see a greasy stain.

WOW! Limeys!

In the past, sailors on long sea voyages couldn't always get enough fresh vegetables and fruit. Many became sick with scurvy, a disease caused by a lack of vitamins. Drinking lime juice, rich in vitamin C, helped to prevent this. This is why British sailors were given the nickname 'Limeys'.

Make sure you eat a balanced diet.

7

What makes me feel hungry?

How do you feel when you are hungry? If your body is not getting the nutrients it needs to give it energy, you may feel tired, or even have a headache. This is because your brain is short of a sugar, called *glucose*, which it uses like a fuel. It is carried in your blood from your stomach to your brain. When the supply runs low, the brain's fuel gauge tells you that you feel hungry. If you then eat or drink something to give you glucose, your hunger will disappear.

Why do tummies rumble when they're hungry?

Because they can't talk!

Filling up

Sugary foods give you a quick energy boost, but you can feel hungry again soon after you have eaten.

Cake

Chocolates

Candy bar   Biscuits

Pure glucose goes straight from your stomach into your bloodstream.

Foods containing starch give a slow, steady supply of glucose. This is better because you don't feel hungry again so quickly.

Starchy foods are digested in long, winding tubes called the *intestines*.

Potato

Bread

Rice

Pasta

Sweet potatoes

Starchy foods also leave you feeling nice and full. Nerves in the wall of your stomach send 'full' messages to your brain.

See for yourself!

1 Try keeping a diary of what you have eaten for two or three days. Make a note of every time you feel hungry. Then think about how long it was since you last had something to eat or drink.

Apple

Granary bar

Grapes

2 Look carefully at what you eat and drink. Does it contain glucose or starch? How soon do you feel full? How long before you feel hungry again?

Banana

Milk

Ice cream

Cheese sandwich

3 Look at your results. You should find that a 'proper meal' containing potatoes, rice or pasta keeps you going. Fatty foods also give your body energy, but they are not so good for keeping your brain alert.

Rice

Potato

Starch makes you feel full for longer.

WOW! Rumbling tummy

If your tummy is empty, you feel hungry. Your brain knows when your body is ready for its next meal, so it makes the tummy muscles tighten. This shakes up the liquid in your tummy, and makes a rumbling sound.

Eating more than you need can make you gain weight!

Why do I get thirsty?

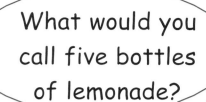

What would you call five bottles of lemonade?

Water is one of the most important substances in our bodies. We cannot live without it. People can survive longer without food than without water. Nearly two thirds of our bodies are made of water. We lose a small amount each time we go to the toilet, breathe, sweat or cry. This has to be replaced so our blood has enough water to keep flowing. When the blood becomes too *concentrated*, we feel thirsty.

A pop group!

See for yourself!

1 Dried beans help to show us how important water is. Take some mung beans and place them on top of a piece of damp paper towel on a tray. Leave them for a few days, keeping them damp and warm.

2 Then take a look. When the beans are dry, they look lifeless. As they take in water, they swell up. After a few days, the beans start to sprout and shoots appear. The water has made it possible for them to begin to grow.

The beans cannot grow because they contain hardly any water.

Dried beans

Damp paper towel

The beans soak up water and begin to sprout.

Little shoots

Keeping a balance!

You replace the water you lose by drinking and eating. Food, especially fruit and vegetables, contains a surprising amount of water.

Food
Drink

Water in

You should drink over 2 litres of water each day.

Breathing
Crying and sweating
Going to the toilet

Water out

If there is not enough water in your blood, the water detector in your brain makes you feel thirsty. Your mouth and tongue feel dry, and you want to drink.

When we are hot, we feel more thirsty.

Wet   Dry

When you drink, water passes through the walls of your intestines into your blood. This makes it more watery, and stops you from feeling thirsty.

Stomach
Blood
Wall of intestines
Water out

WOW!   Thirsty work!

Animals which live in deserts often have to go a long time without water. A camel can go for longer than most, because it stores water in its body. Its hump contains fat which can be used to make water. Some desert rodents never drink – they live on the water in their food.

Make sure you drink enough water every day!

11

Why is food tasty?

Our *senses* tell us about the food we eat. We like it to taste and smell good. Your tongue is covered with tiny bumps. On the sides of these are *taste buds*. They tell you what food tastes like as you chew it. Each bud can sense only one of four flavours – salty, sour, sweet or bitter. Your tongue, however, tastes a mixture of these flavours when you eat. And the scents that your nose smells help you enjoy food even more.

What has buds but never flowers?

Your tongue!

Tastes and smells

Patches of taste buds on different parts of your tongue taste different flavours. As you chew, food mixed with saliva passes over them, and they send a taste message to your brain.

Sweet
Sour
Bitter
Salty

Scent detectors

Nostril

Inside your nose, at the top, are special detectors which pick up scents. When you have a cold, food isn't very tasty because you can't smell it or taste it properly.

See for yourself!

1 Try testing your own taste buds. Start by labelling three cups – 'salt', 'sour' and 'sweet'.

2 Fill the cups half way with water. Add half a teaspoonful of table salt to one, one of lemon juice to the next, and one of sugar to the third.

Salt   Lemon juice   Sugar

3 Place a tiny drop of one flavour on different parts of your tongue (the tips and the edges work best). Try the lemon juice first. Then test the other flavours in turn.

Which part of your tongue tastes the sour lemon juice?

Fiery flavours

WOW!

Have you ever eaten food which contains chilli peppers, like a hot, Mexican salsa sauce? Hot foods, like chilli peppers and mustard oil, make your mouth feel as if it is burning, but hot is not a flavour that your taste buds can sense. You feel it with the sides of your mouth as well as your tongue. They are telling your brain 'Ow, this hurts!'

Not everything that looks good tastes good!

Why does food go off?

If food turns squashy or smelly, we say that it has gone off, or is rotten. It has been changed by tiny living things, called *bacteria* and *moulds*. They feed and grow on food by breaking it down with chemicals called *enzymes*. Food goes off more quickly when kept in warm places where bacteria and moulds grow faster, so we keep food cool in the fridge.

A mouldy elephant!

What's big and green and has a trunk?

See for yourself!

1 Put some pieces of ripe fruit or vegetables into a jam jar, or a small plastic pot, and cover them. Leave the container in a warm place for a few days.

2 Look carefully at the food through a magnifying glass or hand lens. What do you see?

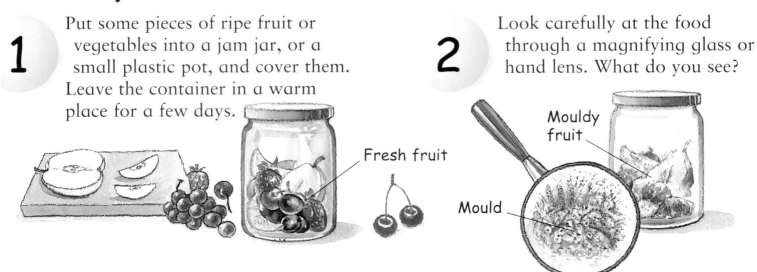

Fresh fruit

Mouldy fruit

Mould

A clean kitchen!

Some bacteria in food produce poisons which make us ill. This is why it is important to keep everything in the kitchen clean.

Always wash raw fruit and vegetables before you eat them.

Do not let raw, uncooked meat touch cooked meat. Bacteria found on the raw meat can be picked up by the cooked meat.

Raw meat

Cooked meat

Always use clean equipment when you are cooking.

Dish-cloths

Sponge

Utensils

Bowls

Make sure you store cooked and uncooked food separately.

Store raw meat on the bottom shelf of the fridge.

WOW! Mouldy medicine!

Mould

Medicine

Mould

An important medicine called penicillin is made from the green mould which grows on fruit. Penicillin is a type of medicine called an antibiotic that helps us to fight germs.

Remember to wash your hands before eating!

15

How do we keep food?

Long ago, people often went hungry when they ran out of fresh food.

Now we have many ways of making food keep for a long time, and can eat what we want all year round. In order to do this, the bacteria, moulds and enzymes which make food go off have to be destroyed or slowed down. There are several ways of doing this. The food can be made very dry, kept cold or mixed with special chemicals called *preservatives*.

Why did the baby strawberry cry?

Because his parents were in a jam!

Stop the rot!

Food will keep for months in a freezer and for days in a fridge, but as soon as the food warms up again it will start to go off.

Fresh peas   Frozen peas

If the food is frozen, bacteria can't grow.

Water can be taken out of food by drying it in the sun, or in kilns or smoke houses. Food can also be freeze-dried.

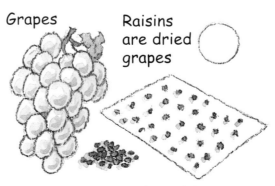

Grapes   Raisins are dried grapes

Bacteria and moulds cannot live in dry food.

Sugar, salt, vinegar and other chemicals are also used to preserve food.

Heating food and storing it in sealed jars or cans will make it last for many years.

Heat kills off any bacteria in the food.

16

See for yourself!

1 Try some different ways of preserving food. Peel two potatoes carefully and then cut them into six chips. Ask an adult to help you with this.

2 Place the chips on three small dishes, and cover one chip with salt, one with sugar and leave one as it is.

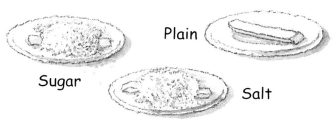

Sugar Plain Salt

3 Put one chip on a piece of paper in an airing cupboard. Wrap two separately in clingfilm, and put one of these in the fridge and one in the freezer.

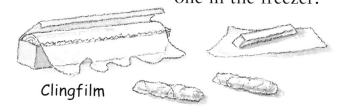

Clingfilm

4 After a week, examine the chips and see which ones have kept the best. Try using the same methods with other vegetables or fruit, and compare the results.

Ice houses

WOW!

Before fridges were invented, people used ice to keep food fresh. An ice house was usually covered by a mound of earth to keep it cool. The ice was brought there in blocks, which would keep cold for up to a year if they were packed tightly in straw.

Check the 'use by' dates on foods in your store cupboard and fridge.

Why does bread rise?

If you look closely at a slice of bread, you can see that it is full of little holes. These made the dough get bigger, or rise, while it was cooking. Cakes also have holes, because they rise too. When the bread dough is being made, the holes are full of gas called *carbon dioxide*. This is made by a tiny *fungus* called yeast. Yeast uses sugars in raw dough to give itself the energy to grow. The gas is what is left of the sugars when all the energy has been used up.

What did the oven say to the dough?

Don't loaf about!

A bubbly mixture

Raw dough rises because the yeast is making lots of gas bubbles. If you have some fast-action yeast in your store cupboard try mixing it with warm water and some sugar.

Warm water

Yeast

Sugar

Risen dough

Little bubbles of carbon dioxide form in the dough while the bread rises.

Baked bread

Bubbles

As the dough gets hot, the gas bubbles start to expand and get even bigger. When the dough is cooked, it sets around the bubbles so that they do not collapse or escape.

See for yourself!

1 Try making your own bread rolls. If you have a packet of yeast, you should find a recipe on the back, or you can use bread mix if you prefer. Follow the instructions carefully.

Bread mix

2 When you have mixed all the ingredients together, cut through the dough carefully and take a look.

Little bubbles forming

3 After you have left the dough to rise, feel the difference. Press it with your finger and see what happens. Then try cutting through the dough again.

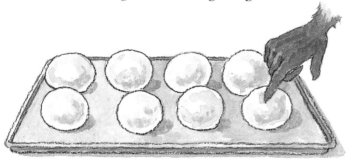

4 Finally, cook your rolls. When they are cool, they should be light and firm to the touch. All the changes in the dough are permanent.

What a gas!

The bubbles of gas in fizzy drinks are just the same as those in bread and cakes – carbon dioxide – but they can escape! They can make your nose feel quite tickly while you are drinking.

WOW!

Don't overcook your rolls or they will burn and turn black!

What happens after I swallow?

Do you ever wonder what happens to your food after you have swallowed it? Like all animals, we need to digest our food. It is one of the things that makes us different from plants. The food we eat needs to be broken down into simpler, smaller substances that our bodies can use. This happens in the gut, or *alimentary canal*, which starts at the mouth and ends at the anus. As the food moves from one end to the other, it is broken down in different ways, and squeezed along by strong muscles in the canal wall.

What goes 'Quick, quick!'?

A duck with hiccups!

See for yourself!

1 To see how your food travels along your alimentary canal, find a large sock and a tennis ball. Put the ball into the top of the sock.

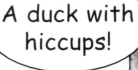

2 Then hold one end of the sock with one hand, and use the other to squeeze the ball along with your hands.

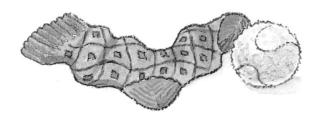

This shows how food is pushed along the canal by muscles in the wall.

Follow your food

You use your teeth to chop or grind the food up into tiny pieces. After swallowing, it is squeezed down a tube called the oesophagus into your stomach.

The stomach is like a stretchy bag which expands to hold food. Thick muscles in its wall mix food up with substances called *acid* and enzymes. These break down the food still further.

The food gradually moves down into a long, thin tube called the small intestine. Here it is digested by more enzymes until nutrients pass through the intestine wall and into the blood.

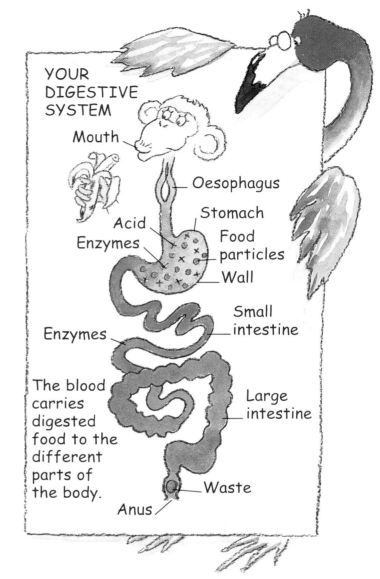

YOUR DIGESTIVE SYSTEM

Mouth
Oesophagus
Acid
Enzymes
Stomach
Food particles
Wall
Enzymes
Small intestine
The blood carries digested food to the different parts of the body.
Large intestine
Waste
Anus

WOW! Stomach stones

Some animals and birds swallow stones to help them grind up the food in their stomachs. Some stones, called gastroliths, have even been discovered alongside dinosaur fossils. They were worn smooth after years of tumbling around inside the dinosaur's stomach, grinding up tough leaves and twigs.

You go to the toilet to get rid of water and food the body doesn't need.

21

Why does a jelly wobble?

Have you ever tried to carry a wobbly jelly? It wobbles because it is made mainly of water. Jellies are held together by gelatine, a *gelling agent* that is used in cooking to set liquids. Gelatine is an animal protein. Agar, another gelling agent, is a jelly-like substance which comes from seaweed. Since they have no colour or taste, gelling agents can be added to sweet or savoury dishes. They are also clear, so if you put pieces of fruit in your jelly, you can see them.

> What wobbles and can fly?

> A jellycopter!

How a jelly sets

When jelly cubes or crystals are mixed with boiling water, they dissolve to make a *colloid*.

While it is still hot, the jelly is runny and can be poured into a mould.

When the jelly is cold, it sets and becomes a solid called a gel. A gel can be made up of almost all water, but the water is trapped and does not run away.

See for yourself! ✋

1 Try making some jellies yourself. Ask an adult to help you with this. Find three small moulds. Follow the instructions on the jelly packet, melting the cubes or crystals in boiling water.

2 Let the jelly cool a little. Pour a small amount of the mixture into each mould. Then top up the moulds with different amounts of cold water and stir well.

3 Leave the jellies to set. Then take a look. If you have used less water than the recipe says, the jelly will be more solid and hold its shape well. If you have used more water, the jelly will be very wobbly.

Right amount of water   Less water   More water

4 Now try making a fizzy jelly. When the jelly is dissolved, allow it to cool and top it up with lemonade or soda water. The bubbles will be trapped as the jelly sets.

Fizzy jelly

WOW!

Collywobbles!

Colloids are not just found in food, they are everywhere. They are in everything that is slimy, sticky or wobbly, such as glue and hair gel. All livings things are made partly of colloids, from bacteria to rubber trees, and slugs to sharks – and even your own body.

Fruit contains pectin, a gelling agent which sets jam.

Why does butter melt?

Cold butter taken out of the fridge is hard. But if you put it in a warm place, it becomes soft enough to spread on bread, and if you heat it in a pan, it will turn runny. Butter melts because it turns easily from a solid into a liquid. A solid is something which stays the same shape and size. A liquid is something which changes its shape to fit its container. Solid butter can stand on a plate, but melted butter needs a container to stop it from running all over the place.

See for yourself!

1 Put a cube of butter, a piece of chocolate, a piece of wax candle and a sugar cube on a plastic plate, and place it by a sunny windowsill or warm radiator.

Wax

Chocolate

Butter

Sugar

Warmth from the sun

2 Leave the plate for an hour, and then look at each one in turn. What changes can you see? Which of them has begun to melt?

What differences do you see?

24

The melting point! ✋

When some solids are heated, you can see them change from solid into liquid. This change takes place at the *melting point*. You can see this when you watch the wax melting on a candle (only do this with an adult).

It doesn't take much heat to melt butter as it has a low melting point. So do many plastics, which is why plastic bowls are not used on the stove or in the oven.

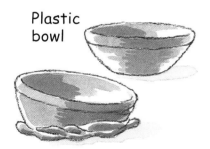

Plastic bowl

Plastic melts

Never put anything plastic on to a hot stove.

The materials used to make cooking pots and pans, like metal, will heat up without melting as they have a high melting point.

Never touch hot pans.

Metal pan

All churned up!

WOW!

Do you know that it takes 20 litres of milk to produce a kilo of butter? Butter is made from milk fat, which is separated from cream by shaking it about, or churning it. In the past, churns were made of wood or stone and operated by hand. It could take up to an hour for the butter to form. It takes a few seconds only with modern machinery.

Wooden butter churn

Don't put chocolate in your pocket - it might melt!

Why does corn pop?

What did the corn say to the crispies?

I'm puffed out!

Have you ever wondered how a small *kernel* of corn can turn into a fluffy piece of popcorn? When a corn kernel is heated in a little oil, it gets hot very quickly. Inside the kernel, there is a tiny amount of water which turns into steam and causes a small explosion. The kernel's tough skin splits as the *starch* inside puffs up to several times its usual size, and lots of air gets into it. Starch is the corn's energy store and when we eat it, it gives us energy too.

Exploding seeds

Plants in the grass family, like maize, wheat and rice, store starch in their *grains*. The grains use this saved energy to sprout and grow into new plants.

When they are hard, grains can be difficult to digest, but we can eat them if they are made light and fluffy.

Wheat

These three plants are called cereal plants.

Maize

Rice

Potatoes store starch in stems under the ground.

Potato

See for yourself!

1 Try popping your own corn. You can buy popping corn to make on the hob of your stove or special packs for the microwave.

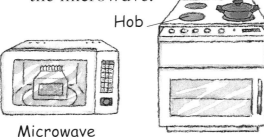

Hob

Microwave

2 Making popcorn on the hob gives you a better chance to discover what is going on, but you must get an adult to help you. You will need some oil and a deep pan with a lid.

Oil

Kernels

3 Follow the instructions on the pack. After the corn has been put in the heated oil, listen carefully. What can you hear?

Pop! Pop!

4 When the popcorn is ready, pour it into a bowl. Compare the cooked corn with the uncooked kernels. What are the differences? Then add a little sugar or salt, and enjoy eating it!

Cooked

Uncooked

WOW! Stiff and starchy!

Starchy powder made from cereal plants and potatoes has many uses. It is used in paper-making and to make glue, and is made into flour for thickening food. The starch used to stiffen clothes before ironing is made from white rice. People who are rather stiff and precise are sometimes described as 'starchy'.

Look out for puffed grains at breakfast time too!

27

Why are pans made of metal?

Most of the pans we use for cooking are made of metals. This is because they are good *conductors* of heat. Metal pans get hot because heat moves through them quickly, which is important if food is to be cooked evenly. Metals are used in pans because they have very high melting points, so they never get hot enough to melt while on the stove. Cooking pots and pans are usually made of iron, copper or aluminium, which are often mixed with other metals to make them strong and hard-wearing.

What did the saucepan say to the orchestra?

I'm a good conductor!

Conducting heat

Before it is heated, a metal pan feels cold to the touch, because it draws heat away from your skin.

The metal conducts heat away from your warm hand.

When one part of the base of the pan is warming, the heat spreads quickly to the rest of it.

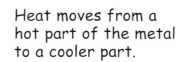

Heat moves from a hot part of the metal to a cooler part.

The heat in the pan is passed on to the food. As the food gets hotter, it cooks.

See for yourself! ✋

1 See how water and chemicals in food attack metals, making them *rust* or *tarnish*. Find two glass jars and some metal objects, such as pieces of cooking foil, iron nails, new copper coins and some old metal cutlery.

Cooking foil

Silver-plated spoon

Iron nails

Copper coins

Stainless steel fork

2 Pour a mixture of water and vinegar into one jar until it is about 2 cm deep. Add a tablespoon of salt and a little beaten raw egg, and stir in. In the other jar put the same depth of water with a tablespoon of bicarbonate of soda and a broad bean pod.

3 Put some pieces of metal into each jar, and leave them to soak for a few days. Then look closely. What effect do you think the changes in the metals will have on any food cooked in them?

Pure iron will rust

Stainless steel should stay the same.

WOW! See your face in it!

Most brand-new pots and pans are shiny. This is because metals reflect light when they are polished. In fact, mirrors were made of metal until the 16th century, when they began to be made of glass. The shine soon disappears from most pans when they are used for cooking. However, stainless steel can resist the damage done by food. It is very strong, and does not rust or tarnish easily, so it keeps its shine.

Be careful not to touch hot metal handles.

Kitchen quiz

 1 How do you have a balanced diet?

    a) By eating one type of food
    b) By eating a variety of foods
    c) By weighing your food before eating it

 2 When does your tummy rumble?

    a) When you're full
    b) When you're thirsty
    c) When you're hungry

 3 What's inside a camel's hump?

    a) Fat
    b) Water
    c) Milk

 4 Where are your taste buds?

    a) In your throat
    b) On your tongue
    c) In your cheeks

 5 What do bacteria and moulds do to food?

    a) They keep it fresh
    b) They make it go off
    c) They make it more tasty

6 What is used to make bread rise?

    a) Yeast
    b) Water
    c) Butter

7 Why do some animals swallow stones?

    a) Because there is no other food available
    b) To help grind up food
    c) To clean their teeth

 8 What does a gelling agent do to a liquid?

    a) It makes it bubbly
    b) It makes it rise
    c) It makes it set

 9 What happens to butter at its melting point?

    a) It changes from a solid into a liquid
    b) It changes from a solid into a gas
    c) It changes from a gas into a liquid

 10 What makes popcorn pop?

    a) Heating it
    b) Freezing it
    c) Soaking it

Answers on page 32

Glossary

Acid
A group of chemical substances that have a sour or sharp taste.

Alimentary canal
The long passage which stretches from the mouth to the anus.

Bacteria
Simple living things with only one cell.

Carbohydrates
Nutrients that supply the body with energy.

Carbon dioxide
A gas found in air, and produced by the body when cells release energy from food.

Cells
The tiny living units which make up plant and animal bodies. There are different types of cells doing different jobs.

Colloid
Formed when a gelling agent is mixed with water.

Concentrated
When a large amount of a substance is mixed in with a liquid.

Conductors
Materials which allow heat to flow through them, without moving.

Digest
To break down food into simple nutrients that the body can use.

Energy
The power needed for doing work or for action.

Enzymes
Special substances made by cells which help break down food. Used by the body during digestion.

Fats
Nutrients that are used to give energy, and to help build the body.

Fungus
A living organism, for example a mushroom or a mould, which is like a simple plant. Some, like yeast, are tiny single cells.

Gelling agent
A substance which forms a colloid when it is mixed with water.

Glucose
A type of sugar which most cells use for energy. Glucose is carried around the body in the blood. It is also used by plants.

Grains
Hard seeds, especially from cereal plants, related to grass.

Intestines
The long, thin, twisty part of the alimentary canal, where food is digested and absorbed. Divides into the small and large intestines.

Kernel
The edible centre of any grain or nut which has a hard outer covering. The grain of a cereal plant.

Melting point
The temperature at which a substance turns from a solid into a liquid.

Minerals
Nutrients needed to make sure the body works correctly.

Mould
Tiny fungus which feeds on the remains of other living things which are decaying.

Nutrients
Substances found in food that are needed to keep living things alive.

Preservatives
Substances which make food keep for longer.

Proteins
Nutrients that are used for growth and repair.

Rust
To become rusty. Rust is a red-brown powder which forms when iron reacts with air and water.

Senses
Parts of the nervous system (the network of cells which take messages around the body) which allow the body to keep a check on what is going on.

Starch
A carbohydrate which stores energy for plants, and is a useful food for animals.

Tarnish
To make a metal dull and discoloured.

Taste buds
Clusters of cells, inside bumps on the surface of the tongue, which sense different tastes.

Vitamins
Nutrients which are found in small amounts in food, and needed by the body to make it work correctly.

Index

Answers to the Kitchen quiz on page 30
1 By eating a variety of foods. **2** When you're hungry. **3** Fat. **4** On your tongue. **5** They make it go off. **6** Yeast. **7** To help grind up food.
8 It makes it set. **9** It changes from a solid into a liquid. **10** Heating it.